IN THIS ISSUE:

tourism.com TATTLER

ISSUE 03 FEBRUARY 2017

PUBLISHER
Tourism Tattler (Pty) Ltd.
PO Box 891, Umhlanga Rocks, 4320
KwaZulu-Natal, South Africa.
Website: www.tourismtattler.com

EXECUTIVE EDITOR Des Langkilde
Cell: +27 (0)82 374 7260
Fax: +27 (0)86 651 8080
E-mail: editor@tourismtattler.com
Skype: tourismtattler

MAGAZINE ADVERTISING
ADVERTISING DIRECTOR Bev Langkilde
Cell: +27 (0)71 224 9971
Fax: +27 (0)86 656 3860
E-mail: bev@tourismtattler.com
Skype: bevtourismtattler

SUBSCRIPTIONS
http://eepurl.com/bocldD

BACK ISSUES (Click on the covers below).

 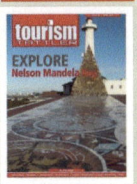 

CONTENTS

EDITORIAL CONTRIBUTORS

Andrew van Heerden
Anthony Whateley
Guy Stehlik
Janet Mackenzie
Leanne van Breda
Lee-Anne Bac
Leon Hugo

Louis Nel
Martin Janse van Vuuren
Samiksha Singh
Tessa Buhrmann
Unathi Henama
Zola Mcaciso

MAGAZINE SPONSORS

ACCREDITATION

Official Travel Trade Journal and Media Partner to:

The Africa Travel Association (ATA)

Tel: +1 212 447 1357 • Email: info@africatravelassociation.org • Website: www.africatravelassociation.org

ATA is a division of the Corporate Council on Africa (CCA), and a registered non-profit trade association in the USA, with headquarters in Washington, DC and chapters around the world. ATA is dedicated to promoting travel and tourism to Africa and strengthening intra-Africa partnerships. Established in 1975, ATA provides services to both the public and private sectors of the industry.

The African Travel & Tourism Association (Atta)

Tel: +44 20 7937 4408 • Email: info@atta.travel • Website: www.atta.travel

Members in 22 African countries and 37 worldwide use Atta to: Network and collaborate with peers in African tourism; Grow their online presence with a branded profile; Ask and answer specialist questions and give advice; and Attend key industry events.

National Accommodation Association of South Africa (NAA-SA)

Tel: +27 86 186 2272 • Fax: +2786 225 9858 • Website: www.naa-sa.co.za

The NAA-SA is a network of mainly smaller accommodation providers around South Africa – from B&Bs in country towns offering comfortable personal service to luxurious boutique city lodges with those extra special touches – you're sure to find a suitable place, and at the same time feel confident that your stay at an NAA-SA member's establishment will meet your requirements.

Regional Tourism Organisation of Southern Africa (RETOSA)

Tel: +27 11 315 2420/1 • Fax: +27 11 315 2422 • Website: www.retosa.co.za

RETOSA is a Southern African Development Community (SADC) institution responsible for tourism growth and development. RETOSA's aims are to increase tourist arrivals to the region through. RETOSA Member States are Angola, Botswana, DR Congo, Lesotho, Madagascar, Malawi, Mauritius, Mozambique, Namibia, Seychelles, South Africa, Swaziland, Tanzania, Zambia and Zimbabwe.

Southern African Vehicle Rental and Leasing Association (SAVRALA)

Contact: manager@savrala.co.za • Website: www.savrala.co.za

Founded in the 1970's, SAVRALA is the representative voice of Southern Africa's vehicle rental, leasing and fleet management sector. Our members have a combined national footprint with more than 600 branches countrywide. SAVRALA are instrumental in steering industry standards and continuously strive to protect both their members' interests, and those of the public, and are therefore widely respected within corporate and government sectors.

Seychelles Hospitality & Tourism Association (SHTA)

Tel: +248 432 5560 • Fax: +248 422 5718 • Website: www.shta.sc

The Seychelles Hospitality and Tourism Association was created in 2002 when the Seychelles Hotel Association merged with the Seychelles Hotel and Guesthouse Association. SHTA's primary focus is to unite all Seychelles tourism industry stakeholders under one association in order to be better prepared to defend the interest of the industry and its sustainability as the pillar of the country's economy.

International Coalition of Tourism Partners (ICTP)

Website: www.tourismpartners.org

ICTP is a travel and tourism coalition of global destinations committed to Quality Services and Green Growth.

International Institute for Peace through Tourism

Website: www.iipt.org

IIPT is dedicated to fostering tourism initiatives that contribute to international understanding and cooperation.

ITB Asia 2017

Website: www.itb-asia.com

25 to 27 October 2017 Marina Bay Sands®, Singapore.

ITB Asia is the leading B2B travel trade event for the entire Asia-Pacific region.

Tourism, Hotel Investment and Networking Conference 2017

Website: www.thincafrica..com

THINC Africa 2017 takes place in Cape Town, South Africa from 6-7 September.

The Hotel Show Africa 2017

Website: TheHotelShowAfrica.com

Thousands of hospitality professionals from around the world will be at Gallagher Convention Centre in Johannesburg from 25-27 June.

The Safari Awards

Website: www.safariawards.com

Safari Award finalists are amongst the top 3% in Africa and the winners are unquestionably the best.

PAN-AFRICAN HEALTH TOURISM CONGRESS 2017
BUSINESS OPPORTUNITY FAIR & EXHIBITION

PAHTC 2017

Website: www.panafricanhealthtourismcongress.com

08-09 June 2017 at the City of uMhlathuze in KwaZulu-Natal, South Africa.

The Pan-African Health Tourism Congress is being staged to address the interests and needs of Health Tourism Stakeholders in Africa.

PROMOTING TOURISM TO
AFRICA
FROM ALL CORNERS OF THE WORLD

Recognised as the Voice of African Tourism, Atta reaches across 22 countries in Africa, showcasing over 530 elite buyers and suppliers of African tourism product.

- Leading role at trade shows around the world
- Networking opportunities
- Industry representation on international commitees & the media
- Interactive platform for information & education
- Daily news service on all aspects of African tourism
- Network of specialist consultants

Join our knowledgeable and experienced membership to increase awareness and visibility of your company

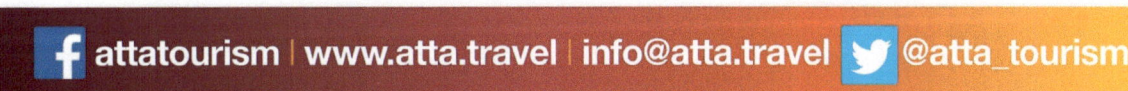

f attatourism | www.atta.travel | info@atta.travel **🐦** @atta_tourism

Lead Sponsor | Working in partnership with Atta

SOUTH AFRICAN AIRWAYS
A STAR ALLIANCE MEMBER

Developing Africa's
Health Tourism
Potential

Health Tourism can potentially provide a lucrative niche market to grow tourist numbers into Africa.
However, reliable information and statistics on this sector from a local perspective are impossible to find.
But this sad state of affairs is going to change as from June this year.

By **Des Langkilde**.

Based on my own research trawling the web, some major practical and image obstacles need to be overcome for health tourism to grow into a mature niche sector in Africa.

Negative perceptions regarding the high incidence of HIV/AIDS and crime are two such obstacles that need to be addressed, from both an international and a local perspective. Studies show that contracting HIV at work is a major fear of African health care providers themselves, while perceptions of crime and security are major factors driving the "brain drain" of African health care professionals to Europe and North America.

The table below shows the number of health care workers in four southern Africa countries (as at 2012) compared to Europe and North America, and compared to the recommended World Health Organisation (WHO) minimum:

Numbers per 100,000 inhabitants			
Country	**Doctors**	**Nurses**	**Health Providers**
Lesotho	5	63	68
Malawi	2	56	58
Mozambique	3	20	34
South Africa	74	393	468
USA	247	901	1147
UK	222	1170	1552
WHO	20	100	228

Source: Médecins Sans Frontiéres, "Help Wanted", P.3

On a more positive note, I found that the potential for tourism entrepreneurs to tap into the growing medical tourism niche lies in government regulations that prohibit doctors and specialist surgeons from directly attracting international patients. For example, South African physicians are ethically restricted from marketing or advertising their services, or to have a photograph of themselves on their website, or to make claims about the quality of their work. They also cannot accept payment for referring a patient to a hotel or travel agent.

These inhibiting regulations provide an opportunity for entrepreneurs to establish facilitation or intermediary services between patients, doctors/surgeons, and the private medical hospitals and clinics. These services could include pre-trip consultations in the patient's home country, connecting prospective patients with African health facilities and surgeons, preparing cost estimates, organising flights and accommodation, and arranging post-surgery tours and activities, such as safaris.

However, to receive a referral fee from doctors as an intermediary, the entrepreneur would need to be appropriately qualified to make medical evaluations and to accept medical liability.

Pan-African Health Tourism Congress 2017

Fortunately, local tourism businesses and entrepreneurs don't need to rely on outdated statistics that I've come across because there's a full blown Business Opportunity Fair, Exhibition and Congress coming to KwaZulu-Natal, South Africa in June 2017.

An impressive line-up of speakers have already been confirmed to present on a diverse range of topics, including The State of Health Tourism in Africa; New Facility Tours; the South Africa Health Tourism Academy; and even the launch of a 'Youth Health Tourism Innovation Hackathon.'

So, if you want to tap into the health tourism niche, the City of uMhlathuze is where you need to be from 8 to 9 June.

For more information visit www.panafricanhealthtourismcongress.com

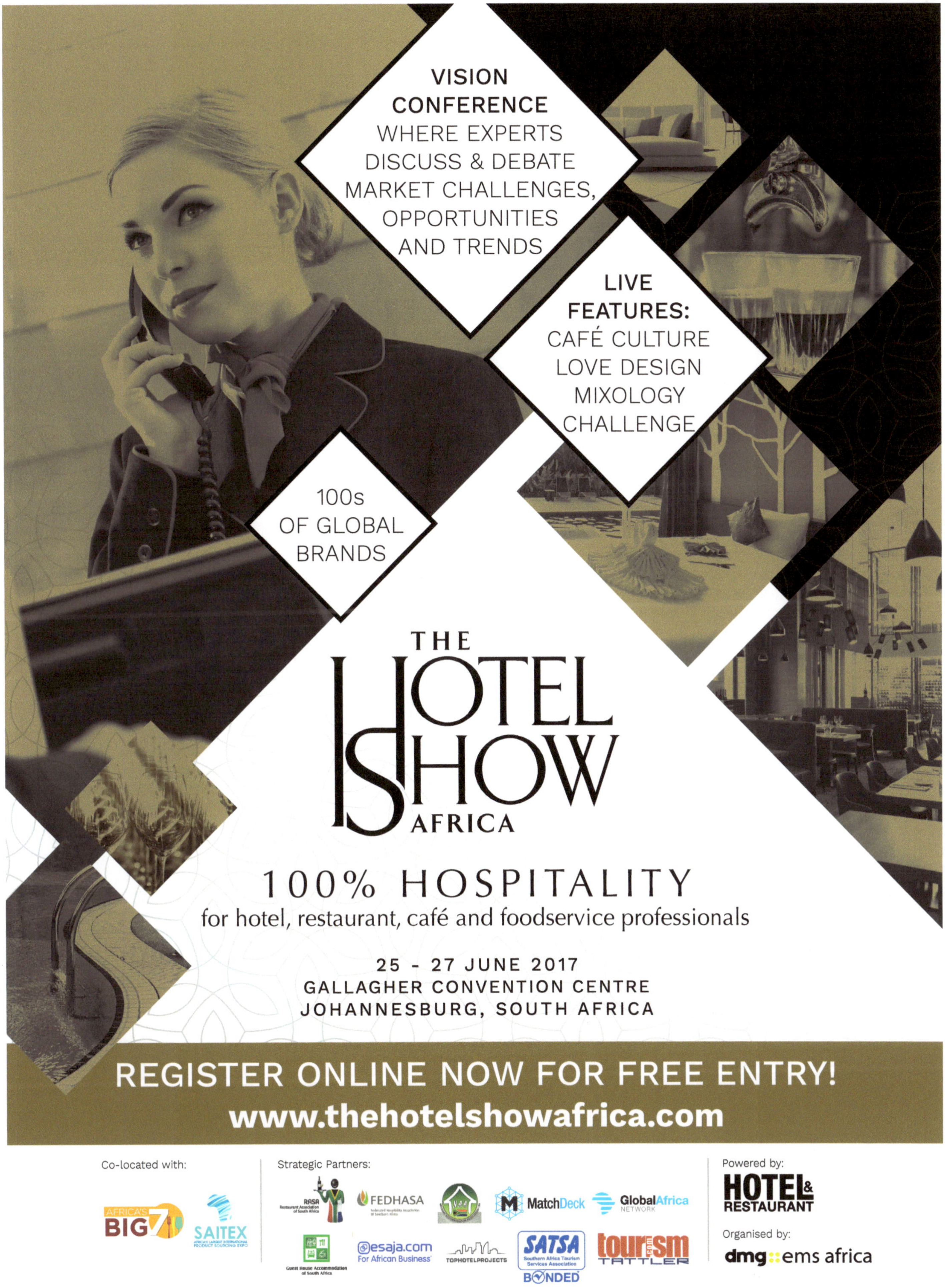
VISION CONFERENCE
WHERE EXPERTS DISCUSS & DEBATE MARKET CHALLENGES, OPPORTUNITIES AND TRENDS
LIVE FEATURES:
CAFÉ CULTURE
LOVE DESIGN
MIXOLOGY CHALLENGE
100s OF GLOBAL BRANDS
THE HOTEL SHOW AFRICA
100% HOSPITALITY
for hotel, restaurant, café and foodservice professionals
25 - 27 JUNE 2017
GALLAGHER CONVENTION CENTRE
JOHANNESBURG, SOUTH AFRICA
REGISTER ONLINE NOW FOR FREE ENTRY!
www.thehotelshowafrica.com
Co-located with:
AFRICA'S BIG 7
SAITEX
Strategic Partners:
RASA
FEDHASA
MatchDeck
GlobalAfrica NETWORK
Guest House Accommodation of South Africa
esaja.com For African Business
TOPHOTELPROJECTS
SATSA BONDED
tourism TATTLER
Powered by:
HOTEL & RESTAURANT
Organised by:
dmg::ems africa

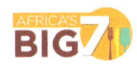

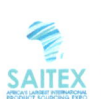

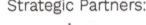

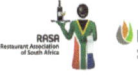

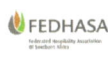

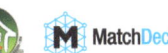

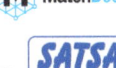

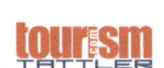

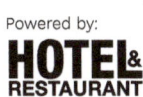

The Cape Town v Pretoria Parliament Debate

#Sona17

During the State of the Nation Address (SONA) on 09 February, President Jacob Zuma set in motion a snowball discourse on the moving of the Parliament to Pretoria away from Cape Town, to reduce costs. The suggested cost for moving Parliament is reported to be R7 billion.

By **Unathi Sonwabile Henama**.

As expected there was more drama at SONA 2017 than we had bargained for, as the national ego was bruised by a spectacle of unfortunates. What happens in Parliament remains a deep sense of embarrassment for the nation which was once a beacon of hope for Africa, now we are a big fat continental joke.

Besides the unfortunates of the day, our eyes must be firmly set on tourism and its developmental potential for the Western Cape. The SONA is always tourism big business for Cape Town. The City of Cape Town which was is the seat of the two houses of Parliament remains the legislative capital city of South Africa. This was an arrangement during the time of the Boer republics, which ensured that Pretoria remains the seat of government whilst Bloemfontein was the judicial capital city, housing the Supreme Court of Appeal.

The adoption of the Constitution, which prescribed that we become a constitutional democracy meant that a constitutional court became the apex court, which would be an arbitrator of disputes, in addition to becoming the official Rottweiler of the democratic project. The Constitutional Court became the highest court, whilst the Supreme Court of Appeal continued a steady stream of judicial tourists that sought to use the court in Bloemfontein.

Getting back to the moving of Parliament issue, Ministers because they must report on progress in Parliament, must have double residential dwellings, two cars, and support staff in Cape Town and Pretoria. Exclusively, all government departments have their headquarters in Pretoria, which means a parliament in Pretoria would mean fewer logistical challenges. The fact that the majority of State Owned Enterprises (SOEs) are headquartered in Pretoria, made the proposed move to Pretoria politically and economically prudent.

In addition, Tshwane Metropolitan Municipality is not just the largest municipality in the world, it houses the second largest concentration of embassies and consulates after Washington DC.

A contestation of ideologies ensued after SONA about the relocation of Parliament, then on August 03, 2016 everything changed. Today Tshwane is governed by a coalition between the Democratic Alliance and the Economic Freedom Fighters, and the Democratic Alliance provided the Mayor after the Local Government Elections. Today, both the cities that house the seat of government (Pretoria) and the seat of the legislature (Cape Town) are governed by the Democratic Alliance, which is the official opposition.

I am of the view that Cape Town would not be in much disagreement about the relocation of Parliament based on the shifting reality of politics. The loss of Parliament would be easily mitigated by tourism as Cape Town is practically a tourism city. The economic value chain of the Western Cape has benefitted immensely from tourism, ranging from the wine routes around Stellenbosch to the film studios outside Cape Town that have recreated South Africa's own Hollywood.

The Western Cape is also a beneficiary of skilled inward migration, from entrepreneurs to cash-rich retirees that are snapping up properties in rural towns around Cape Town, transforming their economies. I call this the Great Trek boomerang.

The Western Cape defined its future by initiating the Cape Town Air Access Initiative that has ensured that Cape Town International Airport welcomed its 10th million passenger in a calendar year. The result was that there were 100 000 additional jobs created around Cape Town, and the indirect impact may be greater. Additional direct flights have been added to Cape Town, and this has continued to ensure that the Western Cape creates jobs, whilst the country has a stubborn 27% unemployment rate.

South Africa as a long haul destination remains challenged by air access which limits the developmental ability and potential of tourism. The lives of the majority of our citizens remain closely friendly to poverty, unemployment and inequality, a reality that remains an unfreedom.

Capetonians have openly embraced AirBNB, reflecting in the largest number of AirBNB listing on the African continent which has increased tourism arrivals and expenditure in the Western Cape. Tourism remains the "new gold" that is the engine of growth in our limping economy. The Western Cape must be congratulated for its progress in advancing the tourism project to achieve the National Tourism Sector Strategy's objective of being in the top 20 destinations by the year 2020.

About the author: Unathi Sonwabile Henama teaches tourism at the Tshwane University of Technology.

**08-09
June
2017**

**Register
Today**

+27 11 040 7352
registrar@mcgroup.co.za

PAN-AFRICAN
HEALTH TOURISM
CONGRESS

BUSINESS OPPORTUNITY FAIR & EXHIBITION

uMfolozi Hotel Casino & Convention Centre | uMhlathuze, KwaZulu-Natal, South Africa

www.panafricanhealthtourismcongress.com

HOST CITY

SUPPORTING PARTNERS

ASSOCIATE PARTNER

MEDIA PARTNER

Market Intelligence Report

SATSA Southern Africa Tourism Services Association

Grant Thornton

The information below was extracted from data available as at **01 March 2017**. By **Martin Jansen van Vuuren** of **Grant Thornton**.

ARRIVALS

The latest available data from **Statistics South Africa** is for **January** to **December 2016*:**

	Current period	Change over same period last year
UK	447 840	9.9%
Germany	311 832	21.5%
USA	345 013	16.1%
India	95 377	21.7%
China (incl Hong Kong)	117 144	38.0%
Overseas Arrivals	2 531 046	18.0%
African Arrivals	7 4672 494	11.2%
Total Foreign Arrivals	10 044 163	12.8%

HOTEL STATS

The latest available data from **STR Global** is for **January** to **December 2016**:

Current period	Average Room Occupancy (ARO)	Average Room Rate (ARR)	Revenue Per Available Room (RevPAR)
All Hotels in SA	65.1%	R 1 181	R 769
All 5-star hotels in SA	65.8%	R 2 177	R 1 432
All 4-star hotels in SA	65.0%	R 1 094	R 711
All 3-star hotels in SA	65.3%	R 925	R 604
Change over same period last year			
All Hotels in SA	2.5%	8.7%	11.4%
All 5-star hotels in SA	4.2%	10.1%	14.7%
All 4-star hotels in SA	3.2%	6.9%	10.2%
All 3-star hotels in SA	3.0%	6.2%	9.4%

ACSA DATA

The latest available data from **ACSA** is for **January** to **December 2016**:

Change over same period last year	Passengers arriving on International Flights	Passengers arriving on Regional Flights	Passengers arriving on Domestic Flights
OR Tambo International	3.0%	3.4%	4.5%
Cape Town International	15.7%	18.6%	5.4%
King Shaka International	20.1%	N/A	7.4%

CAR RENTAL DATA

The latest available data from **SAVRALA** is for **January** to **May 2016**:

	Current period	Change over same period last year
Industry Rentals	1 134 620	-1%
Industry Utilisation	74.2%	3.6%
Industry Revenue	2 375 892 450	10%

WHAT THIS MEANS FOR MY BUSINESS

See editorial on facing page 'Can South Africa Sustain Tourism Growth'.

*Note that African Arrivals plus Overseas Arrivals do not add to Total Foreign Arrivals due to the exclusion of unspecified arrivals, which could not be allocated to either African or Overseas.

For more information contact Martin at Grant Thornton on +27 (0)21 417 8838 or visit: http://www.gt.co.za

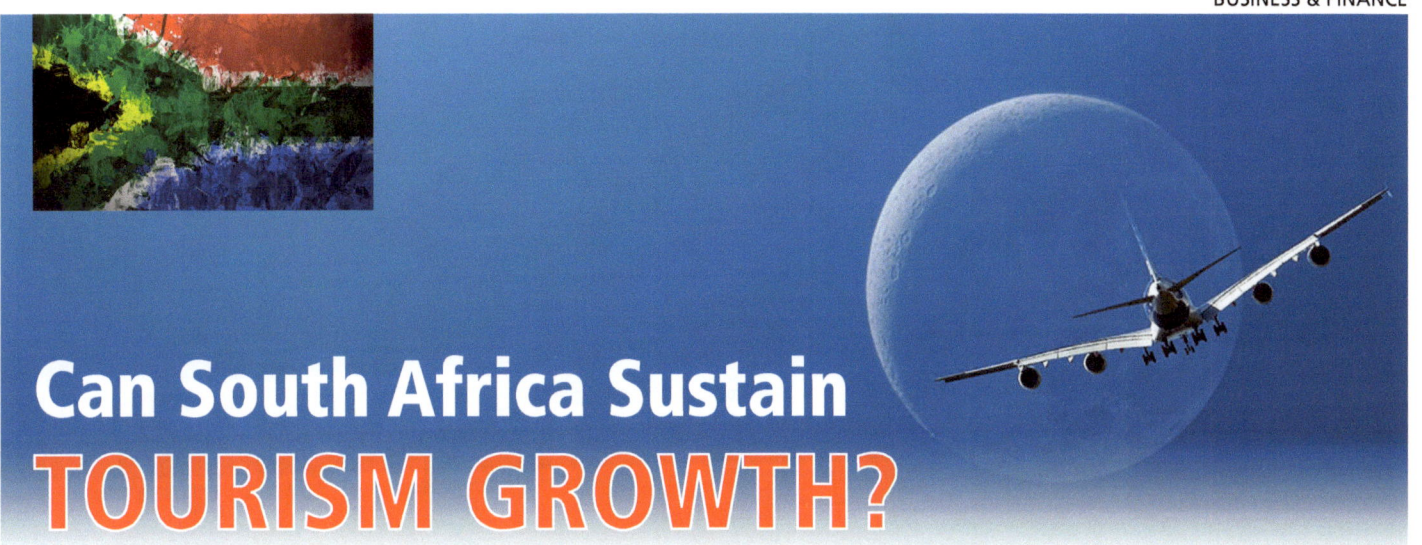

Can South Africa Sustain
TOURISM GROWTH?

By **Lee-Anne Bac**.

While South Africa's 12.8% increase in the number of overnight tourists recorded during 2016 compared to those recorded during 2015 is laudable, further analysis of the data reveals there's still significant work to be done to ensure long-term, sustainable and successful tourism growth.

Looking at Statistics South Africa's release of Tourism and Migration findings for 2016, the 10.04 million overnight tourists that visited our country is certainly impressive and it's a good step in the right direction.

Of the 10 million overnight tourists, 2.5 million were from overseas and the balance, 7.5 million, came from Africa. The number of overseas tourists grew by an impressive 18% compared to 2015 while African arrivals, which comprises the lion's share of tourists recorded during 2016, grew by 11%.

But these figures need to be reviewed in context so that a more realistic picture of South Africa's performance in the tourism industry can be assessed.

It's important to properly consider the decline of nearly 7% of overnight tourists which we recorded during 2015 compared to 2014, with overseas tourists down by nearly 5% during that year.

When analysing tourist arrivals to South Africa, the compound growth figures are very important. In reality, our nation's compound growth in tourist arrivals over the past four years, between 2012 and 2016, is only 3.9% per annum, which is below the long-term worldwide average for international tourism arrivals which is between 4%-4.5%. Fortunately, our compound growth for overseas tourist arrivals during that same period is higher at 4.8%, but this is still regarded as a slow, pedestrian growth figure.

2016's growth did well to 'right-size' the poor growth recorded in prior years when South Africa's tourism sector was performing significantly below the global average.

The red flags in South Africa's bumper 2016 year of tourism

The 2016 tourism data highlights that three of South Africa's key target markets did not perform consistently over the course of the year. Influenced by the Brexit decision mid-year and by the Rand's strength towards the end of the year, the United Kingdom, which is the country's largest overseas source market, only grew by 9,9% for the year in 2016.

China – although achieving excellent growth overall for the year at 38%, in the last quarter this market was actually in decline (-2%). This was probably as a result of South Africa's significant growth in the last quarter of 2015 which was difficult to match in the final three months of 2016.

Similarly, demand from India showed annual growth of nearly 22%, despite only recording a 7% growth in the last quarter of the 2016 year.

The key question, when looking ahead is whether 18% growth in overseas tourist arrivals is sustainable, particularly now that our ZAR Currency has strengthened. When we look at the final two months of 2016, unfortunately it doesn't look like this rate of growth is going to be possible.

The tourism data highlights that overseas tourist arrivals only increased by 13% during November and by 11 % in December last year.

Evidence from last year's data indicates that 2017 is unlikely to see significant growth in tourist arrivals and South Africa is likely to fall back to average levels of growth (around 4% to 5%).

However, there are alternative circumstances which may positively impact 2017's tourism growth:
1. South Africa's ZAR currency once again weakens against major global currencies; and/or
2. Competitive countries are no longer attractive as tourist destinations; and/or
3. Something truly dramatic and different is put into action in order to attract tourists to South Africa.

Only the third point above is within our own control. We need to invest in tourism, just like in any other industry, to make sure that the number of arrivals increase significantly and hence add real value to our citizen economy for the benefit of our people in the form of jobs and business activity.

About the author: Lee-Anne Bac is a Director at Advisory Services for Grant Thornton South Africa. www.gt.co.za

Definitions:
- A tourist is defined as an overnight, foreign visitor, and excludes same-day travellers, transit travellers and work seekers.
- When reference is made to a traveller, this would be foreign tourists PLUS same-day travellers, transit travellers and work seekers An overseas tourist is a visitor who is a citizen of a country outside of Africa.
- An African tourist is a visitor to SA with citizenship of an African country
- African Air-Arrival tourists are African tourists who enter SA via an airport (and not across land-borders).

Come RAIN or SHINE

Making the Most of an African Safari

Tourists come to South Africa for two things – sun and safari. But do they understand that in order to see the Big-5 in their natural habitat it's bound to rain at some point? So how do lodges help guests understand that rain is necessary (and welcome) and how do they keep them enthusiastic when they find that their 3-day safari is going to be a rainy one?

By **Des Langkilde**.

To find out how they make the most of their guest's safari experience on rainy days, I interviewed Rob Gradwell, Managing Director of Lalibela Private Game Reserve in South Africa's malaria-free Eastern Cape province.

"Well firstly, we don't cancel game drives when it rains. Some of the best game sightings that our guests have experienced have been on drives in the rain. Viewing predator species, in particular, is best while rain is falling. The reason for this is that big cats hunt more successfully in the

Modelling the new fleece lined Poncho raincoats equipped on Lalibela's game viewing vehicles are Tania Botha, Kim Fryer and Candice Rusteberg.

This perfectly-timed photo of cheetah in the rain was captured by Irish wildlife photographer Paul Mckenzie.

rain as plains game turn their backs to the angle that the rain is coming from. The rain also dampens sound and decreases smell.

"Secondly, from a guest comfort perspective while on safari in the rain, we have recently replaced Ponchos on our game viewing vehicles with brand new fleece-lined raincoats.

"Our rangers and lodge staff go to great lengths to explain to guests how important rain is in Africa and how essential it is for the flora and fauna. We also brief our guests on the unique photo opportunities that can only be captured in wet conditions. For example, when the earth is wet after a downpour, flying ants burst from the earth in their thousands, while birds take advantage of this as an easy feeding opportunity. Then there's the chance to photograph a rainbow – well worth enduring a few hours' on safari in the rain," says Gradwell.

I then asked Vernon Wait, Lalibela's Marketing Director what guests do on rainy days in-between game drives.

"Like most game reserves and lodges in South Africa, our lodges have comfortable lounges with a wide selection of coffee-table books, novels by popular authors in various languages and board games for guests to enjoy. Then, of course, there is the pleasure to be derived from sitting beside a roaring open hearth fire, while sipping on a South African sherry or Amarula Cream, or a freshly brewed coffee – all of which is provided complimentary as part of our all-inclusive rates at Lalibela."

And what about guests who have young children?

"Mark's Camp has a well-equipped play centre where children are kept busy on dry or rainy days with a number of fun and educational activities, such as rhino T-shirt painting, making African masks, painting, making photo frames, making wind mobiles, and a whole lot more. Also, on a complimentary basis, we provide experienced childminders to take care of children while their parents relax. Special meal times for children under eight years of age, with food more suited to young pallets, also ensures that parents can have more adult time should they choose," says Wait.

I should mention at this point that children have their own game drive accompanied by a Children's Programme Coordinator - read more here.

What pre-trip tips would you give to guests who know that they will be arriving over a rainy period?

"Be Prepared! A lot of the stress about rain on safari stems from what water may do to their expensive cameras and electronic equipment. We recommend that guests bring along a waterproof bag in which to put everything the moment it starts to rain heavily. Although a lot of gear these days can handle a light spatter of rain, it's better to be safe than sorry.

"Also, as with when it is not raining, we encourage our guests to eliminate specific expectations and to be open to anything. Accept the wet conditions and look out for unique sightings that won't be seen in dry conditions. The joy and enthusiasm felt by rangers and lodge staff are difficult to ignore and this often rubs off on guests. It is not uncommon to hear guests talking about their "crazy ranger" who got them to dance in the rain at sundowner time on the game drive," concludes Wait.

From my own experiences of game drives in the rain, I've found them to be exhilarating, as the field guide performs feats of driving on muddy roads, coaxing the Land Cruiser up steep inclines as though he'd been doing it all his life. Of course, he mostly had been. It's all part of the adventure of a safari in the rain. t

For more information visit www.lalibela.net

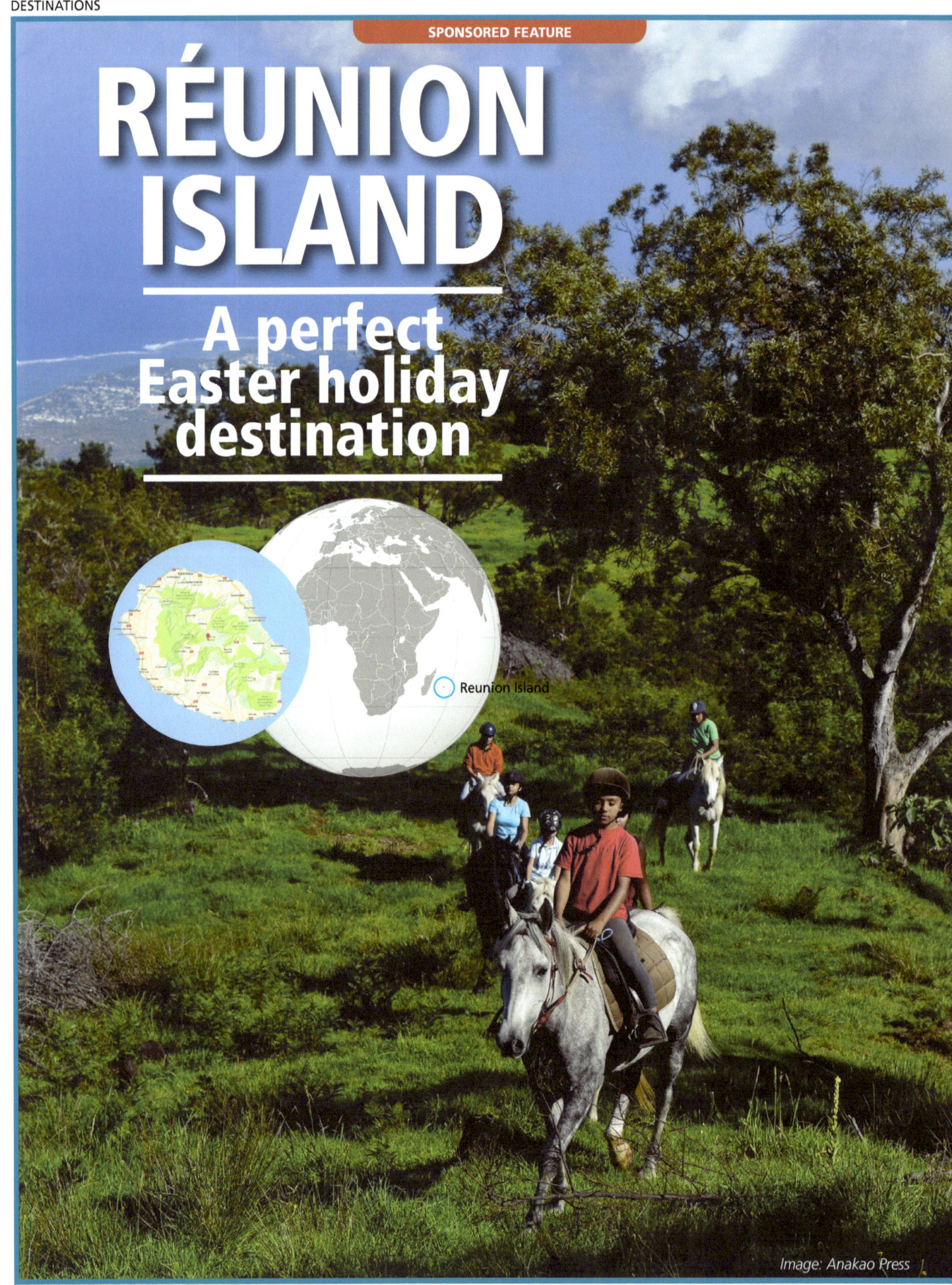

SPONSORED FEATURE

RÉUNION ISLAND

A perfect Easter holiday destination

Reunion Island

Image: Anakao Press

Located in the Indian Ocean, **Réunion Island** can be reached by a quick 4-hour flight on Air Austral from Johannesburg and what's more, South African passport holders do not require a visa for a visit of up to 90 days which makes this island destination a great option for your Easter holidays.

With palm trees rustling in the sea breeze, crystal clear waters, an adventure waiting around every corner and year-round warm weather, you will quickly fall in love with this incredible Indian Ocean Island. This diverse destination boasts an active (but safe to visit) volcano, a warm Indian Ocean lagoon teeming with marine life, over 1000km's of lush hiking trails and a fascinating and engaging local creole culture.

For those who seek a tranquil rest in the most beautiful of surrounds, the island will not disappoint, but for those who like to be active and get outdoors, this tropical paradise offers a plethora of activities.

Take one of the many hikes and marvel at the undulating landscapes formed by years of volcanic activity. Visit Piton de la Fournaise, Reunion Island's famous active volcano. Visitors can even hike to its rim; a fascinating experience. Discover one of the many mountain bike trails and stop at some of the picturesque cascading waterfalls along the route. Try your hand at paragliding, SUPing (stand up paddleboarding), aquahiking or visit giant lava tubes; huge tunnels made in the earth from previous lava flows.

Children will just love a whale and dolphin watching excursion (among other sea creatures such as sea turtles) at Bato Pèi. Aquarium de la Réunion is also a favourite with families, and it's not difficult to understand why, as the aquarium is home to some 500 marine species including seahorses, lobsters and a wide variety of fish species.

The island is also home to fabulous hotels that cater for all tastes and budgets, most of which are family friendly and who's staff love to welcome South Africans to their beautiful island. Depending on where you stay and the age of your children, some of the island's accommodation establishments do not charge for children sharing with their parents in the same room and some offer great fun at their kids' club facilities.

When searching for the ultimate Easter Holidays getaway, look no further than Reunion Island. It will certainly thrill you! There is so much to see and do, you can do a lot or a little, the choice is yours. There is no shortage of memories waiting to be made this Eastertime.

Image: Anakao Press

Image: Emmanuel Virin

Image credit: Gabriel Barathieu

Réunion Island Tourism Board is represented by Atout France in South Africa.

CONTACTS:

 +27 010 205 0201

 reunionisland.za@atout-france.fr

 GotoReunionSA

 @reuniontourisme

 @reuniontourisme

 blog.welcometoreunionisland.com

Image: Anakao Press

The impact of
DROUGHT
on South Africa's Wildlife Environment

By **Andrew van Heerden** and **Anthony Whateley**.

To provide a better understanding of Tourism Tattler's feature regarding the impact of drought on South Africa's game reserves and wildlife environment – and with specific reference to the Hluhluwe Imfolozi Park (HiP) reserve – I have repeated an article written for my newsletter by Tony Whateley, who was doing research in the early days under Ian Player.

In those days the goal was to manage biodiversity first, in the belief that wildlife health will follow. When wildlife health was good it brought in tourists. Today this philosophy has been turned on its head, as influence from Joe Public prevents normal wildlife management. Many of these guys from the old days will happily admit that they made many mistakes, but will quickly remind you that they learned from those mistakes. What beats them up is that outside influence is going to have long-term consequences to the biodiversity. If grassland is replaced by woodland – then there is less capacity to hold the specialist grazers – like the white rhino. In Kruger last year, there were Hippo carcases scattered all over the show. The question we should be asking is if Hippos are dying, then surely Rhinos have also been dying.

The concern expressed by John Forrest in a recent article in the journal Oxpecker that mortality among white rhino in South Africa due to present drought conditions could exceed numbers poached, made me consider the early 1980s drought in Hluhluwe iMfolozi Park (HiP) and additional factors that might now influence mortality.

Drought conditions particularly affecting white rhino in HiP is certainly serious cause for concern, especially when compared with a drought in the early 1980s. Additional factors that are considered to increase the impact of the present drought and that could have far-reaching effects are:

1. a reduction in grazing lawns
2. large numbers of buffalo
3. an increase in large carnivores
4. and siltation of rivers.

1. Grazing lawns

Until the mid-1970s well-utilised grazing lawns in HiP were interpreted by managers as 'overgrazed' areas. The response was to remove large numbers of short grass grazers such as white rhino, wildebeest, warthog and impala. Although widespread seedlings of woody species, such as Dichrostachys cinerea and Acacia karroo were also present in these areas of short grass, where the effects of fire were absent, they were much slower to become established beyond seedling leaf stage due to them being constantly included in grazing pressure. With a consequent reduction in grazers, these woody species often became successful as 'bush encroachment' while still being protected from fire. Over the past 40 years, bush encroachment has gradually and dramatically reduced optimum white rhino habitat in HiP and in many areas been replaced by woodland and in the north of the park, even forest.

Bush encroachment is likely to continue in HiP due to lack of fire and its frequency as a result of drought, further reducing grassland habitat while continuing to change historic savannah landscapes.

In 1972 there was an estimated 2,229 white rhino in HiP and in 1976 1,629. I have no accurate figures for 1980, although, high mortality during this drought took place despite 616 white rhino being removed during 1979 and 1980, which amounted to about a third of the total population. At present, there is about 1,700 white rhino in HiP. This equates to a similar population size of that in 1976 when 40 years ago grazing lawns were far more widespread and annual rainfall was above average during the years 1973-1977.

2. Buffalo

In 1972 there were an estimated 2,195 buffalo in HiP with the first removals taking place in 1974. These early removals were aimed at providing increased fuel in the form of tall grass, which, when burnt, was hoped to arrest unwanted woody growth (bush encroachment) as it was beginning to be realised to be a major problem. However, during 1979-1981, 961 buffalo were removed primarily because of drought conditions. Although I have no population estimates of buffalo for 1979 in 1976 there were an estimated 2,428 in HiP which emphasises the high percentage considered wise to remove prior to and during the drought.

At present, (January 2016), I understand no buffalo have been removed. Despite a severe drought and wise lessons of past management, about 6,000 buffalo exist. With an additional 700 elephant, they will both compete with white rhino for diminishing forage and particularly water, especially in the case of the elephant. (Young elephants were only re-established in 1982).

The carcases of two white rhinos (Ceratotherium simum) – a mother and calf – lie in the bushveld at Hluhluwe-iMfolozi Park. Image: Scott Ramsay.

Regarding elephant numbers in HiP and their re-establishment in 1982, a figure of a maximum of 500 was calculated based on elephant densities and rainfall figures in other parts of southern Africa at the time. With a superabundance of forage in HiP this figure has already been exceeded.

There will be many Zulu who will remember the early 1980s drought when thousands of their cattle died surrounding HiP, and when large numbers of animals were culled in HiP and exported with no benefit to them at all, while simultaneously the South African Red Cross organised food for them.

If, or when, any buffalo are removed from HiP I would hope that this time, providing TB is not a stumbling block, some meat could be distributed to hungry Zulu neighbours.

3. Predation

Large carnivores benefit from the present drought conditions in HiP due to an abundance of easily available food. This will in time further contribute to a decline in many herbivore species as carnivore numbers increase. Over the past 20 years, many herbivores have already declined in numbers due to a combination of loss of suitable habitat (mainly savannah grassland) and predation, while drought conditions will now only exacerbate their plight. This clearly is a classic example of HiP being a 'predator pit' and many large carnivores need to be removed. (Wild dog were only re-established in 1980 as juveniles and played no part in the early 1980s drought. While lions numbered about 100 at the time).

4. Siltation of rivers

Continued siltation and reduced flow in all the large rivers in HiP is yet another problem during low rainfall years. This is because deforested catchments outside of the park can no longer easily retain water while being prone to heavy grazing and soil erosion. Although the term 'perennial' was used to describe some of these water courses 40 years ago, 'seasonal' is now a more applicable description. The loss of riverine forest in the south of the park during cyclone Demoina in 1984 has created wide shallow water courses where the riverine forest is unlikely to become re-established due to seasonal flash flooding and unstable banks.

While accepting that tourism plays an essential role in the continued survival of HiP, drought conditions certainly accentuate the limited size of this island-like park. It reveals the need to reduce popular game viewing species such as white rhino, buffalo, elephant and lion.

Anthony Whateley ex NPB.

About Andrew (Bugs) van Heerden: Bugs publishes The Conservation Imperative – an informal, unaffiliated organisation created for the purpose of promoting the philosophy of sustainable utilisation of wildlife in accordance with the IUCN's sustainable use policy across the full spectrum of wildlife management practices. Bugs is also the owner of a game farm in KwaZulu-Natal, and owns shares in a private game reserve in Botswana.

About Anthony Whateley: Anthony is a retired Natal Parks Board game ranger and author of '**I Think of Africa**' - a memoir of his life in the bush, his colleagues, zoological and botanical work, close encounters with big game, and problems facing managers and scientists.

Taking Action Against
PLASTIC

Global campaign to stop plastic pollution presented at Rio Earth Summit. Title: 'Just because you can't see it, doesn't mean it isn't there.' Image: Ferdi Rizkiyanto.

To kerb the disastrous environmental impact of plastics, a new report released by the World Economic Forum provides a tangible plan for the global plastics industry to take action across all types of plastic packaging.

In just over half a century, plastics have become pervasive throughout the economy, due to their versatility and cost-efficiency. Yet alongside clear benefits, today's plastics system has significant drawbacks. This need not be the case, however.

As much as 20% of plastic packaging could be profitably reused and 50% of plastic packaging could be profitably recycled if improvements are made to design and after-use systems. The remaining 30% of plastic packaging (by weight), equivalent to 10 billion garbage bags per year, is currently by design destined for landfill or incineration, and requires fundamental redesign and innovation; otherwise, it will never be recycled.

This is according to a 2017 report published by the World Economic Forum, in collaboration with the Ellen MacArthur Foundation and McKinsey & Company.

The report titled 'The New Plastics Economy: Catalysing action' provides a tangible plan for the global plastics industry to take action across all types of plastic packaging, to design better packaging, increase recycling rates, and introduce new models for making better use of packaging.

Continuing with the current business-as-usual scenario, projected growth in plastics production could lead to the oceans containing more plastics than fish (by weight) by 2050, and the entire plastics industry could be consuming 20% of total oil production and 15% of the annual carbon budget.

Looking at the full range of plastic products (not just packaging), concerns have been raised about the potential negative impact of some substances, such as certain phthalates in PVC and bisphenol A in polycarbonate, on society and the economy.

Plastic packaging – the focus of the New Plastics Economy initiative – is plastics' largest application, representing 26% of the total volume.

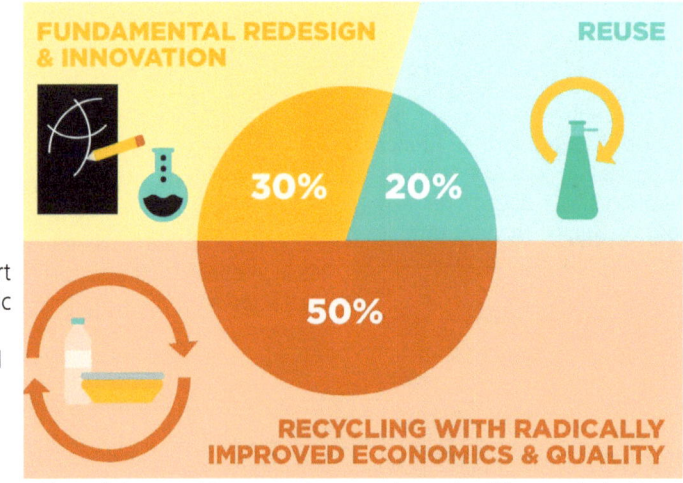

Three distinct transitions strategies to accelerate the shift towards the New Plastics Economy (share of plastic-packaging market by weight).

PLASTIC OCEAN

192 COUNTRIES BORDERING THE ATLANTIC, PACIFIC, INDIAN OCEANS AND MEDITERRANEAN AND BLACK SEAS PRODUCED **2.5 BILLION METRIC TONS OF SOLID WASTE** IN 2010. AN ESTIMATED **8 MILLION METRIC TONS OF PLASTIC** ENTERED THE OCEAN THAT SAME YEAR.

Ocean Conservancy

Ocean Conservancy's Trash Free Seas Alliance estimates that 8 million metric tonnes of plastic enter the ocean each year. www.oceanhealthindex.org

Most plastic packaging is used only once and 95% of its value, estimated at $80 billion-$120 billion annually, is lost to the economy after its initial use. Additionally, plastic packaging, which is particularly prone to leakage into the environment, generates negative externalities, degradation of natural systems and greenhouse gas emissions, that have been valued conservatively by UNEP at $40 billion. For these reasons, plastics and plastic packaging have gradually morphed from a fringe to a mainstream issue.

The global momentum for a plastics rethink has triggered a broad group of stakeholders to act. Policy-makers are introducing landmark legislation worldwide, affecting plastics and plastic packaging, with examples from 2016 including:

- further national regulations on single-use plastic bags in Indonesia, Colombia, and Morocco;
- a ban on non-biodegradable plastic cutlery, cups and plates in France;
- a ban on EPS packaging in San Francisco.

In November 2016, citizens of California approved Proposition 67, which prohibits grocery and other stores from providing customers with single-use plastic takeaway bags. This is in addition to more 130 regulations, at a city level and countywide, across 20 states, governing plastic packaging in the United States alone.

Importantly, the EU Commission aims to publish a strategy on plastics as part of its Circular Economy Action Plan by the end of 2017. The NGO community is also intensifying its efforts, as shown by the #breakfreefromplastic movement. Launched in September 2016, the movement, which aims for a future free from plastic pollution, grew to over 500 member organisations in just a couple of weeks.

Academic experts are increasingly studying plastics and their impact on the economy and society. Aside from plastics leakage into the ocean, the impact of substances of concern in plastics (not just packaging) is one active area of research. Besides polymers, plastics contain a broad range of other substances, with some of them raising concerns about complex long-term exposure and compound effects on human health.

Download the full report at:

www3.weforum.org/docs/WEF_NEWPLASTICSECONOMY_2017.pdf

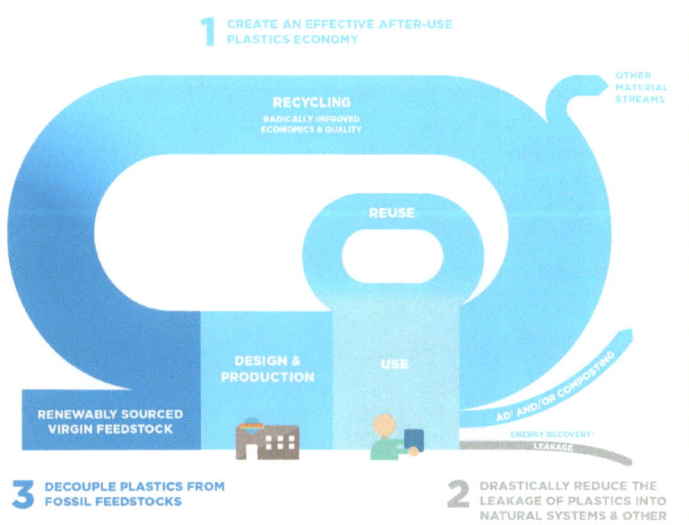

The New Plastics Economy and its three ambitions. Source: The New Plastics Economy – Rethinking the future of plastics.

Does South Africa Need Two B2B
TRADE SHOWS?

Does the tourism industry in South Africa benefit from the concept of B2B trade shows, and if so, is the presence of two major travel trade shows in an emerging market like South Africa sustainable?

By **Des Langkilde**.

The Stats

South Africa's international tourist arrivals surpassed 10 million last year, 13 percent more than 2015 *(see the stats on page 08)*.

The reason for this growth can be attributed to a number of factors. South African Tourism's global marketing campaigns, aimed at attracting more foreign tourists to the country, has no doubt, contributed to this growth. However, there have been numerous initiatives driven by the private sector in the tourism industry that has also contributed to this growth.

Whilst global marketing campaigns to promote positive brand awareness of South Africa is important, other tactical strategies resulting in actual tourists visiting South Africa is also important. The current challenges that are negatively impacting on South Africa's brand image include issues of corruption, education crisis, and leadership uncertainties, among others. These issues cannot be addressed through advertisements promoting the positive experiences of the country. Direct contact with the global trade needs to be made to educate and assure them that South Africa is still an attractive destination to visit.

Trade shows or Business-to-Business (B2B) exhibitions, by their very nature, encourage dialogue between businesses seeking opportunities (buyers) and businesses promoting their products and services (sellers). It is well documented that for business to succeed, the need for face-to-face meetings is critical and B2B trade shows provide the platform for businesses to engage with each other and more importantly, to conclude business deals.

The Global Association of the Exhibition Industry (UFI) estimated that the value of the global exhibition industry in 2015 was worth over USD 55 billion, translating to 680,000 full-time jobs. UFI's Global Barometer shows that the exhibition industry is geared for further growth in 2017. According to UFI, visitors and exhibitors spend around USD 109 billion annually attending exhibitions. 50% of this benefits the tourism industry, which consists mainly of the accommodation, transport, food and beverage and shopping sectors. Research undertaken by the Association of African Exhibition Organizers (AAXO) estimates that in 2015 the exhibition industry contributed R74,9 billion to South Africa's economy, translating to more than 150,000 jobs via direct, indirect or induced spend.

Clearly, there is ample evidence to show the value of the exhibition industry and its impact on tourism.

But does South Africa need two major B2B trade shows to sustain growth? Let's take a look at each.

Indaba

The annual Tourism Indaba, owned by SA Tourism, has been South Africa's iconic leisure travel trade show. Hosted in Durban over the past 26 years, the Tourism Indaba was the only B2B travel trade show held on the African continent. Since its inception Indaba continued to experience steady growth in terms of the number of international buyers and exhibitors that the event attracted. However, since 2012, there has been a decline in participation with many in the industry complaining that "the event's iconic energy was lacking".

Statistics from the Indaba website reveal a 27% decline in exhibitor numbers between 2012 (1,437) to 2016 (1,049), and a 42.37% decline since 2010 (1,820). During this period international buyer numbers also declined from 2,518 in 2012 to 1,531 in 2016 representing a decline of 39%.

These declines often result in lost business opportunities for the tourism industry. The industry, therefore, called on SA Tourism to change the focus of Indaba aimed at aligning its format to global trends and exploring partnerships with global players in the travel trade industry.

WTM Africa

Recognising the opportunity to take advantage of the growth in the African tourism industry and the need to address industry concerns for a global travel trade show to be launched in Africa, Reed Exhibitions entered the South African market. With over 3,700 employees across 40 countries, owning over 500 events in 43 economic sectors – Reed's global travel portfolio of 22 international travel trade events – would have benefited SA Tourism. Various attempts to forge a partnership with SA Tourism to grow Indaba apparently failed, and the result was the launch of a new travel trade show focused on the leisure market in Cape Town in April 2014 known as World Travel Market (WTM), Africa.

The WTM brand is a global brand owned by Reed Exhibitions and is strongly associated with the global travel industry. Reed's decision to launch this brand in SA reaffirms the significant global interest in the South African and African tourism markets. According to Sugen Pillay, Commercial Director at Reed Exhibitions, WTM Africa has grown significantly since its launch in 2014 with exhibitors increasing from 370 in 2014 to 646 in 2016 translating to an increase of 42%; trade visitors increasing from 2,132 in 2014 to 3,050 in 2016 (30% increase); and buyers' club members increasing from 279 in 2014 to 653 in 2016 (57% increase). In 2015 it was estimated that USD 333 million worth of business was signed at WTM Africa, which no doubt contributed significantly to the 10 million foreign tourists to South Africa.

Sustainability

Given the aforementioned stats, one could argue that the combined effect of Indaba and WTM Africa sustained numbers at 2,184 buyers and 1,695 exhibitors for 2016 (similar to Indaba's 2013 figures, prior to WTM Africa's 2014 launch), so in effect, there has been very little change. However, the number of duplicates (who visited as buyers or exhibited at both trade shows) is an unknown factor.

The concern, though, is that exhibitors are raising questions about the affordability of participating in both events. Comparing the cost of exhibiting at the two trade shows, floor space at Indaba 2017 is R2,553 per sqm and R3,326 per sqm at WTM-Africa 2017. I doubt that there are many SME tourism business owners who can afford nearly R53,000 for a 3x3-meter stand at both shows, not to mention the cost of transporting their stand from Cape Town to Durban – a distance of 1,363 km by road – just 3 weeks later.

Review

As we operate in a free market economy, competition is healthy and gives the consumer more choices. However, as Indaba is owned by SA Tourism – a government controlled DMO mandated to promote South Africa globally – should it be involved in the business of managing exhibitions? This question was articulated in the SA Tourism Review conducted by a panel of experts in 2015, and I quote: *"SA Tourism should seriously consider handing over the management of Indaba to an independent operator, given that industry is now actively and successfully operating in this space (as evidenced by WTM Africa), and the drain that Indaba places on SA Tourism resources."* Read the 'SA Tourism Review Report' article here.

Although SA Tourism did invite proposals for a strategic partner to grow Indaba and Meetings Africa, the process appears to lack transparency. As far as I am aware, the reasons for not going ahead have never been released and therefore requires closer scrutiny.

Conclusion

The statistics from both events show a clear picture – B2B trade shows do make a significant contribution to the country's tourist arrivals, to the economy, and to job creation. But looking ahead to 2018, does South Africa still need two trade shows? What are your thoughts? Email editor@tourismtattler.com

DIABETES
Are You At Risk?

Early diagnosis of diabetes is important if complications are to be prevented or delayed. If you are over 35 and have any of the risk factors highlighted in this article, you should be tested every year.

Who is at risk?

Risk factors for developing Type 2 diabetes include the following:

- Being aged 35 or over
- Being overweight (especially if you carry most of your weight around your middle.
- Being a member of a high-risk group (in South Africa if you are of Indian descent you are at particular risk).
- Having a family history of diabetes
- Having given birth to a baby that weighed over 4kg at birth, or have had gestational diabetes during pregnancy
- Having high cholesterol or other fats in the blood
- Having high blood pressure or heart disease.

A simple finger-prick test at your local pharmacy or clinic can diagnose the likelihood that you may have diabetes within a minute.

How is diabetes treated?

Having diabetes need not mean the end of a normal, healthy life. People with diabetes need to first accept the fact that they have the condition and then learn how to manage it.

This takes commitment and perseverance. The goal of diabetes management is to bring blood glucose levels into the normal range, that is, between 4-6mmol/l.

How is diabetes managed?

There are various aspects of good diabetes management.

Education: Knowing about diabetes is an essential first step. All people with diabetes need to learn about their condition in order to make healthy lifestyle choices and manage their diabetes well. Join your local branch of Diabetes SA and attend courses in diabetes self-management. Make an appointment to see a Nurse Educator who will set you on the path to good diabetes management.

Healthy Eating: There is no such thing as a 'diabetic diet', only a healthy way of eating, which is recommended for everyone. However, what, when and how much you eat play an important role in regulating how well your body manages blood glucose levels. It's a good idea to visit a registered dietician who will help you work out a meal plan, which is suitable to your particular lifestyle and needs.

Exercise: Regular exercise helps your body lower blood glucose, promotes weight loss, reduces stress and enhances overall fitness and enjoyment of life.

Weight Management: Maintaining a healthy weight is especially important in the control of type 2 diabetes. Make an appointment to see a registered dietician who will work out a meal plan to help you lose weight.

Medication: People with type 1 diabetes require daily injections of insulin to survive. There are various types of insulin available in South Africa. Type 2 diabetes is controlled through exercise and meal planning and may require diabetes tablets and\or insulin to assist the body in making or using insulin more effectively.

Lifestyle Management: Learning to reduce stress levels in daily living can help people manage their blood glucose levels. Smoking is particularly dangerous for people with diabetes.

About Diabetes South Africa

Diabetes SA (DSA) is a registered NGO/ non-profit organisation and public benefit organisation and has been in operation for over 47 years.

DSA has Section 18A(1) Approval and is a member of the International Diabetes Federation, which represents 147 diabetes organisations in 121 countries.

Appeal for Donations

DSA is a small organisation when considering the huge demand for services, a demand that is increasing as more and more people are diagnosed with diabetes every day. DSA is run mainly by volunteers with only a handful of paid employees. To continue expanding the programmes and services offered, DSA needs support and funding from individuals, government and private corporations.

Donations will receive a tax receipt, which is tax deductible to the donor in accordance with the Income Tax Act. The organisation also has BEE Level 4 Contributor status.

For more information visit *www.diabetessa.org.za* or call +27 (0)21 425 4440 or email: *margot@diabetessa.org.za*

Common Symptoms of
DIABETES

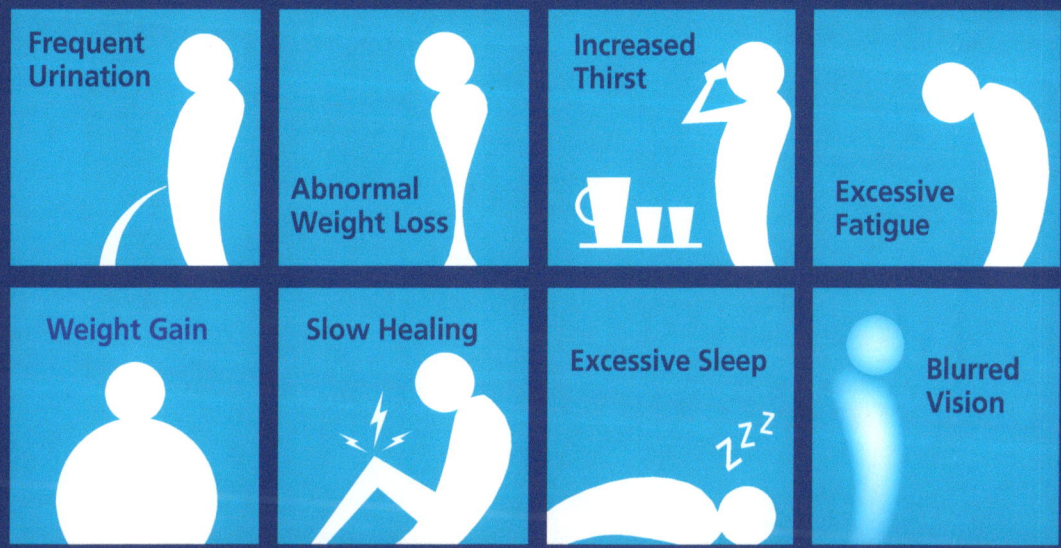

Frequent Urination

Abnormal Weight Loss

Increased Thirst

Excessive Fatigue

Weight Gain

Slow Healing

Excessive Sleep

Blurred Vision

If you experience any of these symptoms, you may be diabetic.

422 MILLION
adults have diabetes
That's 1 person in 11

Prevention is better than cure.
Don't wait until it's too late. Get self-care advice today.

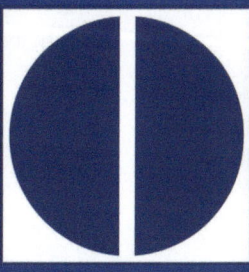

Tel: +27 (0)21 425 4440
national@diabetessa.org.za

Diabetes
South Africa

Facebook.com/Diabetes.South.Africa
www.diabetessa.org.za

The Importance of Hotel ENTERTAINMENT

At a recent hotel industry function, I was asked which was THE best hotel I have ever stayed at. This has been a common question over the years and one that has an easy answer. It's also a question to which I enjoy watching the reactions to my reply.

By **Guy Stehlik**.

I suppose I am expected to mention the likes of 'The Ritz Carlton in Shanghai' or 'The Lanesborough in London'; however, my decision is not based on six-star facilities or Michelin-rated restaurants, nor is my verdict based on white-gloved waiters or state-of-the-art cocktails. My choice is based on one thing – how the place made me feel.

I was very fortunate as a youngster to escape the doom and gloom of the Cape Town winter, whisked off to one of the properties that my dad worked at: a highlight for me and my family. I will never forget how it felt, from the anticipation of our stay to the absolute joy and delight during our stay, to the disappointment of it all ending. San Lameer on the KwaZulu-Natal south coast gets my vote. The best hotel in the world!

Why?

The true secret to hospitality – be it at your home, in your office or at a hotel – comes down to "how did we make you feel". I can honestly say that I don't recall the quality of the food or the style of the décor in the room, but I definitely remember the smell of the buffets and braais on the terrace, the sight of the Zulu dancers and the sound of the African drums. The intoxicating entertainment, leaving children and adults gasping in delight. I remember the staff and how they treated me, the hands-on manager – Mr Andre Steyn – noticeably involved, evident even to a young boy of 8. We had a blast, and we created memories. There was so much stuff to do! Kiddies and teenagers were catered for and considered with respect. Adults had an entertainment program too, so everyone was happy.

Resort management is a tricky thing, believe me. And we have, at times, found ourselves wanting. It seems that modern-day resorts, apart from the likes of Umhlanga Sands and Sun City, don't necessarily give enough consideration to their entertainment. Making sure that they offer high-quality entertainment, across all ages and in a safe and secure environment, should be a key driver.

San Lameer was always busy, so you were never the only kid. We made friends at the disco and 'played it cool' with the DJ (who was always top quality, shipped in from Durban). We had a games room, with the latest and greatest version of Donkey Kong or Space Invaders, and a pool table that didn't veer off to the left top pocket. We played volleyball on the beach and couldn't take our eyes off the lifesavers. On rainy days we were bundled off on shopping trips to Margate (I kid you not!) The new arrivals or shy little ones hiding behind mom's skirt were enticed by a team of entertainment specialists, drumming up support for activities and getting everyone in on the fun. Our parents could rest their weary souls, knowing that their kids were going to have a blast.

The result: a no-brainer for your next family holiday. We would already start nagging my mom in the car returning to the airport if we could go back to San Lameer. And when she agreed, we wanted to know when! How soon?

Resort hotels have an opportunity in this country to reinvent themselves: what a terrific sales tool that entertainment could be! I do understand the challenge – the cost and organisation of entertainment in times when the hotel is not busy. My retort? Just begin! Remember, the Pied Piper gathered the children of Hamelin one by one.

About the author: Guy Stehlik *is the CEO and founder of BON Hotels. With an innate enthusiasm and dedication to the hotel industry, Guy's innovative and creative approach has ensured a successful and impressive career spanning many years as an hotelier and hotel owner.*

For more info visit www.bonhotels.com/blog

Can you justify your Fixed-term Contracts?

It is important for employers to ensure that they are able to justify the grounds for fixing a limited duration of employment and that there is full compliance with the relevant provisions of the LRA insofar as ensuring the protection of employees and avoiding any adverse orders of the Labour Court.

By **Zola Mcaciso** and **Samiksha Singh**.

Since the implementation of the amendments to the Labour Relations Act (LRA) in 2015, there have been several interesting judgments dealing with the justification for concluding a fixed-term contract of employment.

One such case involved two employers, who contracted with their client to provide various services until 2021. The employers then contracted a number of employees, on fixed-term contracts of employment, in order to carry out these services to their client. The fixed-term contracts of employment included a clause which provided for automatic termination in the event that the commercial contract between the client and the employers prematurely terminated. By inclusion of this clause, the employers were of the view that these employment contracts constituted fixed-term contracts of employment.

During November 2016, the client terminated the commercial contracts with the employers by giving them one month's notice. The employers then relied on the automatic termination clause in the fixed-term contracts of employment and terminated the employment relationship with their employees.

The Union representing the employees, launched an urgent application to the Labour Court in terms of s189(13) contending that the employees were dismissed for operational requirements as envisaged by s189A of the LRA (retrenchments), and accordingly the employers were under an obligation to consult with the employees prior to termination of the employment relationship. In its application, the Union requested the Labour Court to order reinstatement, therefore forcing the employers to engage in consultation with the employees as envisaged in s189 of the LRA.

The employers argued that the employees were employed on fixed-term contracts, which was terminable on the occurrence of a specified event, namely the early termination of the commercial contract with their client, and as such s189 and 189A of the LRA was not applicable. The employers further argued that the fixed-term contracts of employment were governed by s198B of the LRA, which provides that employees may be employed on fixed term contracts or successive fixed-term contracts of employment for longer than three months if the nature of the work is for a limited duration or that the employer can demonstrate a justifiable reason for fixing the term of the contract.

The Labour Court found that the employers failed to demonstrate justifiable reasons as the fixed term contracts of employment were not for a specific project that had a limited duration. The client terminated its contract with the employers, which resulted in the automatic termination of the fixed-term contracts of employment. There was no evidence that a specific project had come to an end as envisaged by s198B of the LRA (being one of the justifiable reasons set out in the LRA).

The Labour Court reaffirmed the position that employers cannot terminate an employment contract at the behest of a third party as this undermines the employee's right to fair labour practice entrenched in our Constitution. Consequently, the Labour Court ordered the reinstatement of the employees. 🇹

About the Authors: Zola Mcaciso and Samiksha Singh represent Cliffe Dekker Hofmeyr's Employment Practice.

The impact of PINTEREST on copyright laws

By **Leanne van Breda** and **Janet Mackenzie**.

The traditional realm of copyright is being tested in a world where "liking", "retweeting", and "pinning" have become part of everyday life.

Copyright vests exclusively with the creator of the work or in the copyright holder. These rights are considered economic rights and may be licensed or assigned to third parties by way of agreement, which attach to the works even after the assignment of rights to a third party. The creator must, therefore, always be credited.

Where an image is "pinned" directly from the original source, the link to the source will be attached to the "pin", visible to all other Pinterest users. Where an image has been downloaded from its original source and uploaded to Pinterest, however, the Pinterest user is provided with the opportunity, and not the requirement, to provide the link to the original source. Needless to say, there are many unsourced images being "repined" on a daily basis without royalties being paid to the copyright owner.

Pinterest itself is protected against any claims of copyright infringement in terms of s512 of the Digital Millennium Copyright Act of 1998, meaning that a copyright holder's sole remedy against Pinterest is to lodge a copyright complaint with Pinterest who will then investigate the complaint and remove the image from its platform. The copyright holder will then need to institute direct action against any Pinterest user who has infringed his/her copyright in order recover any damages suffered as a result. 🇹

About the Authors: Leanne van Breda & Janet Mackenzie represent Cliffe Dekker Hofmeyr's Convergence and New Media practice.

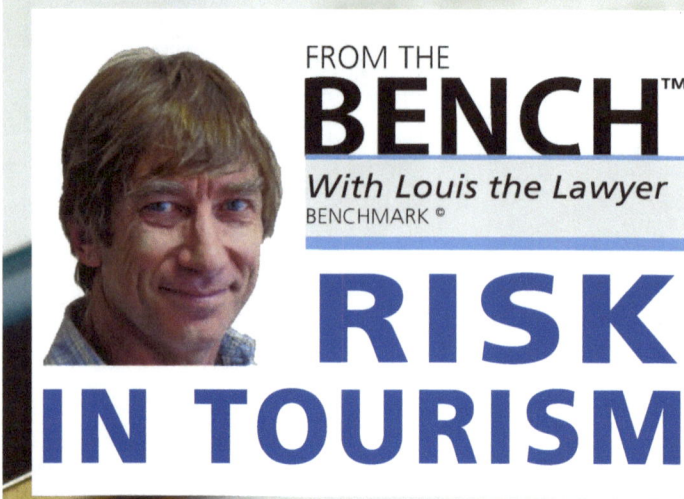

FROM THE
BENCH™
With Louis the Lawyer
BENCHMARK ©

RISK IN TOURISM

THE LAW: CONTRACTS

- Part 27 -

The Role of: Service Level Agreements

Alternative Dispute Resolutions (Cont'd)

I ended Part 26 (FEB 2017) by stating that arbitration becomes the method of resolving a dispute if parties to the dispute choose that method of problem-solving at the time, or if it is a clause in an agreement governing the relationship that gave rise to the dispute.

Another alternative, to be preceded by wording to the effect that the MDs or CEOs of the businesses concerned will first try and resolve the matter, is to refer to the rules of the AFSA and to allow for AFSA to appoint the arbitrator if the parties cannot agree.

Arbitration does offer the following advantages:

1. **Flexibility**: e.g. choice of arbitrator, venue, timing and procedure

2. **Costs**: This may however sometimes be a perceived benefit as you still have to employ an attorney and more often than not counsel (advocate) as well. This benefit will only really materialise if the parties maximise the benefits of arbitration e.g. the informality, the expertise of a correctly chosen arbitrator and limiting the use of expert witnesses.

3. **Speed**: This is a very real benefit, especially the parties can agree on deadlines e.g. for the filing of pleadings (arguments) and you have a strong arbitrator. This benefit can be enhanced even further if the parties meet beforehand to define the issues and exchange relevant documents (which meeting may or may not be presided over by the arbitrator).

4. **Confidentiality**: The matter is not heard in an open (public) court (See brand management above).

5. **Finality**: Arbitrator's finding is final and can only be attacked on basis of misconduct or gross irregularity.

6. **Equity**: Arbitrator can make an award relying on equity rather than on the 'letter of the law'.

7. **Relationship**: The chances are the relationship between the parties is less likely to be damaged by arbitration than litigation.

Arbitration could, however, be linked to the following disadvantages:

1. **Costs**: this can, in fact, be as high as litigation if benefit 1 above (esp. the procedure) is not fully maximised.

2. **No appeal**: i.e. a bad award is not appealable.

Mediation has the same benefits as arbitration but not the disadvantage of high costs – the latter is materially lower and more manageable.

There are four main ADR bodies in South Africa, details of which can be obtained via the Internet i.e.
- AFSA
- The Arbitration Forum
- The Association of Arbitrators
- The CCMA: The Commission for Conciliation Mediation and Arbitration

I trust the above will give you a better grasp of ADR, assist you in preparing more effective contracts and reducing your legal bills! **t**

This series of articles explores the legal aspects associated with the risks of operating an adventure tourism business, with specific relevance to the legal framework applicable to South Africa.

Part 9

By 'Louis The Lawyer'

Image courtesy of Canopy Tours

ADVENTURE TOURISM
from a legal perspective

Summary: **Part 1** provided definitions for the term Adventure, while **Part 2** looked at risk in terms of Nationality of Participant, Service Providers, Bookings, and Terms & Conditions, and **Part 3** covered Indemnity and Requirements of the CPA. **Part 4** explained why signage must go in hand with a sound indemnity and waiver form, **Part 5** dealt with Duty of Care in relation to Negligence, Omission, and Relationship, and **Part 6** concluded with Acceptance of Risk and Insurance. **Part 7** started the checklist for Risk Identification & Management, and **Part 8** continued the checklist.

RISK IDENTIFICATION & MANAGEMENT CHECKLIST FOR ADVENTURE SPORT OPERATORS (Conclusion)

Insurance

Insurance is a crucial part of risk management. Essentially there's the operator's own cover which may apply to the business assets as well as participants and then the participants may well have arranged insurance themselves via the travel agent with whom they booked their trip.

You need to ascertain whether they (Participants and SP) are insured and if they are you want to see copies of their policies, ascertain who they are insured by and that premiums are (and will be kept) up to date.

The nature of their cover could impact on yours but it is better to have your own cover ('belt & braces') than to 'fall between two stools'.

The medical aspects and emergency evacuation should be addressed especially where the activities take place in remote locations.

The insurance aspect should extend to claims and complaints handling – The recently formulated and published Consumer Goods & Services Ombudsman Code of Conduct makes the latter a prerequisite (More about this later).

Service Provider Terms & Conditions

I mentioned SP T&Cs in Part 8 – in each instance you need do to ascertain whether the SP has T&Cs, obtain and peruse a copy and also give it to your insurer and lawyer. Compare them with yours and ascertain how they are enforced. When were they drafted and when last have they been re-assessed? How are the SP T&Cs enforced: e.g. do pax sign them personally or does their (overseas) booking agent sign it (on their behalf? NOT recommended!)? The same applies to SP indemnities and one of the aspects to address is the extent to which the SP T&C & indemnity covers you.

Ultimately, once you have carried out the above series of checks on your own business and the SP you use, enter into a detailed agreement with the SP.

I will address in next issues and in more detail the following: CPA regarding intermediaries and absolute liability; The EC regulations and POPI, and the Consumer Goods and Services Ombudsman Code of Conduct. 🄣

To be continued in Part 10 (April).

Online Marketing for your small Business

The internet has expanded dramatically in the last decade and is becoming a part of every aspect of daily life. Businesses are recognising that their customers spend a considerable amount of time online and are coming up with innovative ways to market and promote their services on the web. Where should you start?

Learning about the internet is the first step

Before you dive into online marketing, the first step you should take is to learn about the internet world. If you are unfamiliar with online behaviour, lingo and tools, you could do considerable harm to your brand image. Masha du Toit, an experienced internet teacher, says that web skills are highly sought after in our interconnected world, and that no forward-thinking businessperson can afford to ignore the internet. Create a solid foundation of web know-how so that you can build appropriate, responsive and lucrative online marketing campaigns. You can achieve this through the Tattler's Tourism Support Sevices facility (see pages 14 - 15 in this magazine) or by taking an online course in the subject.

Basic principles

Once you feel comfortable online, you can start to plan your online marketing strategy by keeping the following basic principles in mind.

- **Create a holistic strategy.** To be truly successful online, you need to create a varied and interconnected strategy across various platforms. For example, there's no sense creating a beautiful website if you neglect to optimise it for search engine and don't spread the word on social media and in emails. Each marketing channel must feed into and build on the others.

- **Only use what you need.** Some people who venture into online marketing try to do it all – they open profiles on every social network, build websites, send emails, launch SMS campaigns – but never take the moment to consider what is best for their brand and target audience. Only use the tools that are appropriate to your image and that you know your customers are also using.

- **Start slow.** Online marketing takes years to perfect and optimise, so don't be afraid to start with one or two tools and expand from there. Doing too much at once will create added stress and raise your expenses, and will usually mean that you cannot devote yourself to any one aspect fully.

- **Don't focus on the hard sell.** Very little of internet marketing involves proper advertising and hard selling; it's usually more about subtle approaches, community building and public relations. Pushiness and blatant self-promotion are generally not appreciated online. When you get these aspects right online, the sales will follow naturally.

There are many aspects or approaches that you can take when marketing your business online. The most popular ones are creating a social space for your customers, creating an online "office" and getting word out about your brand.

Building a community

Social media platforms like Facebook and Twitter are perhaps the best-known online marketing tools and are ideal for social branding. Social branding is the process of marketing your brand in an online social space. It's all about creating brand equity, increasing awareness and fostering loyal communities.

Social media are less about making direct sales and more about building a community of fans and followers. Social networks are used for chatting, sharing information and photos, writing recommendations and passing on links to friends. They are a place for having a conversation with your customers, responding to questions, addressing complaints, offering special deals and sharing media and offers.

In basic terms, social branding involves creating profiles on social media websites and filling them with brand-related content that is geared towards reinforcing the business' desired brand image. It's not enough to create a Facebook, Twitter or WordPress account, however; you need to engage daily, meaningfully and appropriately with your social networks.

Conversations, good and bad, will happen around your brand regardless of what you do. Therefore, it's vital that you participate in them and steer them in the right direction. Participating involves both acting – creating and adding content, links and information – and reacting – listening and responding to customers.

Having an active and engaging social media strategy is a large element of building a reputable brand image. If customers see your activity frequently, they will begin to trust your business over the long term. Your business will appear supportive, legitimate and enduring. While it won't happen instantly, this goodwill will build and will become incredibly valuable.

Creating your online office

Before the advent of the internet, companies needed an office or some sort of physical presence to interact with customers. This included the need for high rental fees and reception staff, and severely limited the scope of the business. Online, the picture is very different. Many companies now have a virtual presence, and some exist as a website alone – their "office" is a digital address on the web.

Customers are comfortable interacting with a business through the digital portal and often find it more convenient, efficient and rewarding. They can examine the product offerings, do research, read testimonials and contact the company in one place, without having to travel physically.

A website is the cornerstone of any marketing strategy – all of the adverts, social media, email messages and so on must direct to one central space to be truly effective. It is possible to replicate the intimacy, personality and interaction of the physical office through a website, and it allows the business to market itself globally. The market reach potential is endless – but make sure that your infrastructure can handle doing business internationally.

Having an attractive, professional and informative website is essential. It is the definitive source of information about your business, and a place where you can include the most up-to-date information available.

Spreading information

The internet seems to be an endless database of information, so getting the word out about your business requires careful thought and targeting. Conveying your message over the clutter can be difficult, so it is very important to be original and visible. The more precisely you can target your information to people who are interested in your business, the more successful you will be in generating sales. A few ways of doing this are creating content, optimising your website and sending email marketing campaigns.

Content and search engine optimisation (SEO) go hand in hand. Creating content involves writing website copy, articles, blog posts, brochures and any other written or multimedia information about your business. SEO is the process of optimising this content so that the right people can easily find it by using a search engine like Google. SEO is a highly specialised skill, but you can learn to do some basic SEO yourself.

Setting up a regular email newsletter is an excellent example of how to keep your current customers up to date on information about your business and to inform them of special offers, discounts and deals. Email is an excellent way to reach people because you can target your recipients very specifically; you can gather data from your own customers and find other likely people to approach online. If you include good content and offers that your customers enjoy, it will be easy for them to pass the email on to their friends and grow your customer base for you.

Measuring your effectiveness

Perhaps the biggest benefit to marketing yourself online is being able to monitor and track your efforts accurately. The web offers a wide variety of analytics tools that can help you understand your customer by tracking and reporting on their online behaviour on your website. Analytics tools can show you, for example, how many people are visiting your site, which pages are the most popular, and how they spend their time on your page. Measuring your key performance indicators gives you valuable insight into your online marketing return on investment. For example, seeing how many people opened your marketing email and clicked on the link to your website will immediately tell you if your approach was successful. The immediacy of online marketing means you can test and adapt your strategy to better reach your audience.

Remember the risks

While online marketing is easy, accessible and very powerful, it also comes with its own set of risks. The biggest one is that an online presence leaves you exposed and transparent – everybody on the internet can potentially see your content, comments and strategies, so any misstep will be magnified considerably. While a small typo on your website will be excused, the aggressive comment you leave on an unhappy customer's Facebook page will not. The adage "think before you speak" should always be on the forefront of your mind.

The other big risk is legal trouble, especially in light of South Africa's Consumer Protection Act. It is never acceptable to spam or harass anyone online, so be careful with any direct marketing that you do. Customers should always have the option of opting out of email communication, for example. Breaking the law when marketing is not only ethically unsound, it also makes your business look bad.

TRAIL
Accreditation

GREEN FLAG TRAILS QUALITY TRAIL

HIKE
CANOE
HORSE
KLOOF

Tourists want reassurance. For this reason, hotels are star graded, beaches are awarded Blue Flag status, and clean and safe trails are Green Flag accredited.

By **Leon Hugo**.

Ten years ago, adventure tourists had no means of assessing an advertised trail's quality standard, risk potential or difficulty in terms of fitness level required. Now they do!

The Green Flag Trails accreditation system (implemented through Hiking Southern Africa) is not a grading system that promotes one trail as being superior to another. It's a scientifically based, accurate third-party assessment that allows tourists to make informed decisions, knowing that they will get what is being promised, and will be assured of a good trail experience.

Green Flag assessments take the following aspects into consideration:

- **Service and facilities:** Car park, stiles, bridges, access road, sanitary facilities.
- **Safety:** At huts and along the trail and an assessment of how risk is managed.
- **Accommodation:** Classification of accommodation types (Luxury, Comfortable, Basic or Rustic)
- **Environment type**: Pristine, Rural, or Semi-urban.
- **Environmental responsibility**: Conservational status.
- **Difficulty rating**: Objectively calculated in terms of energy required.
- **Technical classification**: Walk, scramble, or climb.

Why Quality Trails Matter

1. Benefits to trail users

By hiking, paddling, riding or climbing Green Flag Trails, trail users are assured that they will have a satisfying experience as they will find the trail character and facilities exactly as advertised, safe and well managed. Personal and community enhancing values include:

- Appreciation of nature and cultural heritage.
- Value-for-money by making an informed choice based on trustworthy information.
- Improved health and wellness.
- Improved social values with families and friends.
- A well-managed, safe, and relaxed experience.

2. Benefits to trail managers and owners

Assurance that in cases where their clients lodge legal claims for compensation for injuries sustained, they will be regarded favourably as having provided a responsible recreational product to the public – assessed by an outside professional body. Note that this does not imply full indemnity against all mishaps.

With the Green Flag logo as a quality assurance mark, owners are adding credibility to their trail and making trail users aware that they have their enjoyment of a quality trail experience at heart. This approach will expand the trails market by ensuring satisfied

trail users, which in turn results in sustainable income and support for the trail.

With the assurance that a trail is safe and under responsible management, trail users will not feel apprehensive to visit foreign environments and countries.

Through its unique audit procedure, Green Flag accreditation identifies, acknowledges and rewards those trails that demonstrate and practice responsible management, in contrast to trails which negate the enjoyable experience and safety of hikers and responsible environmental stewardship.

Green Flag Trails provides the necessary guidelines to trail managers for maintenance and monitoring procedures of their trails so as to help conserve the natural heritage where trails pass through.

3. Benefits to the environment

Green Flag Trails ensure the effective use of land. Large tracks of land on privately owned farms and government land lies idle as it is regarded as "unproductive ground". These areas are often excellently suited for hiking: mountain slopes, deep valleys, indigenous forests, floodplains, riverine stretches, even marshy land. Hiking is a non-consumptive utilisation of resources and provides an extra, low-investment, income to land owners.

The concept of eco-efficiency is a recent extension of the sustainability concept –

The author training the auditing team in the Himalayas (Annapurna Panoramic Trek) – 1st Green Flag trail in Nepal (October 2016).

multiple-use of resources without degrading any of them – thus adding value. Responsible hiking trails are ideally suited for this approach.

Green Flag monitors the extent of exotic and invasive plant species, pollution, erosion and all other environmental problems.

4. Benefits to economy and eco-tourism

As a capacity building service for government officials and private individuals, the Green Flag Trail system delivers a service to the tourism industry by assessing and providing feedback on the quality of the services rendered by trail owners/managers as to the:

- Marketing and management of their trails.
- Safety through a risk assessment study.
- Degree of environmental responsibility.
- The monetary value of trails to the tourism sector of the economy, including the outdoor equipment industry (financial benefits).
- Job creation through training. Green Flag Trails runs annual training courses in trail development, which includes:
  - planning,
  - building, and
  - auditing of trails.

How to gain Green Flag Trails accreditation

There are three steps to the audit process:
- Preliminary Self-Audit.
- Full-fledged Green Flag Certified Audit .
- Re-audit (2nd audit).

Step-by-step details can be viewed online: *www.greenflagtrails.org/application-process/*

Which trails are Green Flag accredited?

There are currently (as at March 2016) 40 hiking trails in South Africa that have Green Flag Trail status, with at least another 40 pending accreditation. Countries such as Peru, Nepal, Swaziland, St Helena, Namibia and Mozambique all have Green Flag trails.

The Green Flag Trails system was developed at the University of Pretoria (under the leadership of Prof Leon Hugo). It is underwritten by the non-profit organisation, Hiking Southern Africa (HOSA) and is being implemented by all large trail provision agencies in South Africa: SANParks, KZN-Ezemvelo, Cape Nature and SAFCOL (Komatiland Forests and Cape Pine: MTO) as well as major urban municipalities

such as Johannesburg and Pretoria (Tshwane) and many private landowners.

Internationally, the most well-known trails that have received Green Flag status include the Inca trail in Peru; the High Peak trail on the island of St Helena; and the Otter trail in South Africa. An eight-day section of the Anapurna trail in the Himalayas is in the process of being certified. Nepal has formally started a programme of auditing their Great Himalaya trekking trails in 2016. 🇹

An alphabetical list of all accredited Green Flag Trails (Day Walks and Multi-day Trails) can be viewed at: *www.greenflagtrails.co.za/hiking-trails*

About the author: Professor Leon Hugo is the Chairman: Quality Control committee at HOSA (Hiking Orgnisation of SA).
Cell: +27 (0)82 578 3023 / Office: (0)28 388 0036
leonhugo@vodamail.co.za
www.greenflagtrails.org
www.hosavosa.co.za

VEHICLE REVIEW

The Awesome AWD
MAZDA CX5 Akera
2.2L Automatic

By **Tessa Buhrmann**.

With kerb appeal to satisfy even the most sophisticated of motorists, one wouldn't be surprised if this SUV's 'off-road' abilities were somewhat limited. When Mazda gave Tourism Tattler an opportunity to review the CX-5 2.2L DE Akera AWD Auto – the flagship vehicle in the CX-5 range, we jumped at it and I headed off for Amakhosi Safari Lodge in KwaZulu-Natal.

My thoughts were 'a gravel road or two, some good sandy cornering and a few pics in the bush'… but clearly my hubby and Amakhosi's GM had other thoughts – 'we need to put the Mazda through its paces' I was told. And that we certainly did!

At this point, we had already established that this really good looking SUV (that had somewhat stolen my heart) was perfect on the open road. And that the 2.2L DE Auto with SKYACTIV technology would comfortably rise to the occasion when acceleration was required, thanks to the two-stage turbocharger that maximises power and efficiency. We had appreciated its luxury interior featuring leather trim, electrically adjustable driver's seat and of course cruise control as well as the MZD-connect display system (smart-phone friendly and with navigation system), reversing camera and awesome 9-speaker Bose sound system.

The Mazda CX-5 was the first vehicle to introduce the KODO-Soul of Motion design into the South African market back in 2012 and has been a popular choice with SUV buyers – and in 2015 an updated version with advanced technology, improved functionality and refined interior and exterior design was released. The cosmetic updates on the Mazda CX-5 2.2L DE Akera AWD Auto, like the bold new front grille, new-generation LED headlamps and gunmetal 19-inch alloy wheels certainly give the CX-5 a heightened appeal.

In addition to its built-in SRS airbags, safety features include Lane Keep Assist, Dynamic Stability Control, Traction Control System, Electronic Brake-force Distribution and Emergency Brake Assist.

With Mazda having taken care of the vehicle's safety, it was up to the guys to check the spare wheel, organise the recovery vehicle (which had me a little nervous) and plan the route.

We were exceptionally privileged to take the Mazda CX-5 Akera onto roads normally reserved for game viewing vehicles – the robust kind that is seriously equipped with off-roading (and river-crossing) abilities! The words 'we're going to cross the Mkuze River…' had me wondering how I would ever explain to Mazda Southern Africa that I had 'drowned' their brand new vehicle!

I needn't have worried. The Akera handled the terrain exceptionally well considering its eye-catching rims and relatively low ride height. From river crossing to hill climb, through ditches and over rocks (albeit small ones…), driven with care and some off-road experience this soft-roader will for most people's applications meet their requirements splendidly.

So what did the guys think?

The hubby: "The automatic gearbox is really nice, with the ability to slow right down, crawl up hills and have great control negotiating uneven road surfaces – you don't need a low ratio gearbox as it deals with the challenging terrain really well. Really impressed with the vehicle…"

The Amakhosi's GM: "The suspension is really comfortable and it dealt with the terrain really well… very impressed, I must say!"

And my impressions: 'Generally I'm not that big into SUV's, but this one was definitely a keeper! So I'm looking forward to the opportunity of driving the slightly smaller Mazda CX-3, so watch this space."

For more information visit www.mazda.co.za

About the author: Tourism Tattler correspondent **Tessa Buhrmann** is the editor of **Responsible Traveller** magazine. *www.responsibletraveller.co.za*

FAST FACTS:

Price:	R533,400 (2017 - Incl VAT)
Engine:	2.2-litre 4-cylinder Diesel
Compression ratio:	14.8 : 1
Maximum power:	110kW/129kW
Maximum torque:	380Nm/420Nm
Fuel consumption:	5.9 l/100km (combined)
Warranty:	3-year unlimited kilometre factory warranty
	3-year roadside assistance
	3-year service plan
	5-year Corrosion Warranty.

www.ingramcontent.com/pod-product-compliance
Lightning Source LLC
Chambersburg PA
CBHW041306180526
45172CB00003B/990